# THE MOST IMPORTANT THING I KNOW

✳

COMPILED BY LORNE A. ADRAIN

MJF BOOKS
NEW YORK

Published by MJF Books
Fine Communications
Two Lincoln Square
60 West 66th Street
New York, NY 10023

*The Most Important Thing I Know*
Library of Congress Catalog Card Number 99-74467
ISBN 1-56731-353-1

Published by arrangement with Andrews McMeel Publishing and
Cader Books

Editorial:    Verity Liljedahl, Jake Morrissey, Dorothy O'Brien,
              Nora Donaghy
Design:       Charles Kreloff, Orit Mardkha-Tenzer
Proofing:     Jennifer Moon
Legal:        Renee Schwartz, Esq.

Manufactured in the United States of America on acid-free paper

MJF Books and the MJF colophon are trademarks of
Fine Creative Media, Inc.

10   9   8   7   6   5   4   3   2   1

# Contributors

To L. Allan W. Adrain
and M. Lorraine Adrain
for showing me how to care
and for so much more
than I could ever express.

# Introduction

On my seventh birthday, I watched the inauguration of John F. Kennedy and was inspired by his challenge: "Ask not what your country can do for you, but what you can do for your country." As I grew, I was inspired and challenged closer to home by the words and works of everyday life and the people in my life. My parents, alone in a new country and raising eight children, still made time to be dedicated community volunteers. My scout leaders from Troop 1 Warwick taught us simple lessons of great value: to leave a campsite cleaner than we found it and to do a good turn daily. In college, my brothers at Theta Chi (Greek for "helping hand") raised money to buy Christmas gifts for poor children. From the many people who patiently and selflessly built bridges for me, I learned how to build bridges for others.

We learn important things every day from all kinds of people. I thought it would be fascinating and inspiring to capture the thoughts of some of our most respected leaders. I wrote to people and asked each to share a personally inspiring thought on leadership, excellence or service. I asked for handwritten responses to leave an intimate and enduring impression. The response I received was extraordinary, both in volume and in content.

When it was time to write an introduction, I wondered how on earth I could add something to the thoughts I had collected. I came to see the book as my way of participating in the common responsibility to share ideas and wisdom, in the hopes of improving the human condition.

People need to hear messages that honor the dignity of human potential. I hope this collection of heartfelt thoughts will underscore the simple truths of a successful life and ignite inspiration, courage and hope. As this book illustrates, it is not what you achieve that is important, but the underlying spirit in everything you attempt. The belief that something is worthwhile and possible, the willingness to risk failure and overcome resistance in pursuing it, the commitment and hard work required to make it happen, and the eagerness to pursue new and greater challenges creates a spirit with which we each can change the world in wonderful ways.

One of my favorite places is Long Pond in Hope Valley, Rhode Island. From the top of an 80-foot cliff I can throw a pebble into the water and watch it ripple seemingly forever. Just as that pebble creates an expanding ripple on the pond, our daily thoughts, words and deeds ripple through time and space. Life is the story of those ripples. I hope that in some small way, this collection reminds us to enjoy the world and each other and to make good ripples every day.

LORNE A. ADRAIN
JANUARY, 1997

*Adrain is a graduate of the Harvard Business School and the University of Rhode Island. He owns a national insurance, benefits, and estate planning practice. He is an active community leader and lives in Providence, Rhode Island with his wife, Ann Hood, and their children Ariane, Sam and Grace.*

# Acknowledgments

All royalties from this work will be given to charitable organizations in Rhode Island to support and celebrate leadership, excellence and service in my community. Thank you for buying the book and helping me to realize visions for my community. I hope that in return, these thoughts help you to realize your dreams. The spirit in my life and work has been nurtured by my extraordinary family, friends and mentors, "the giants on whose shoulders" my visions and values evolved. To my wife Ann Hood, whose love and belief make anything possible and whose daily interest in the book was invaluable and fun. To my dear children Ariane, Sam and Grace, who have enriched me with purpose and allowed me to appreciate the glorious gift of life itself. To Mom and Dad and to my brothers and sisters, Ross, Mark, Lindsay, Lorraine, Anne-Marie, Alyn and Lee, who have provided countless lessons and a foundation from which I have found the courage to create. To Fred and Kathleen Ramsperger, my grandparents, aunts, uncles and cousins. To Sue Aldrich, Jon Feinstein, Ted O'Sullivan, Jim Azzinaro, Mike Falvey, Charlie Anthony, Tom Greene, Jim Meegan, Dave Whalley, Rick D'Alfonso, Jeff Jacober, Jim Buehler, Kim Polak, Mike Matone, Vince Agliata, Howard and Ruth Rosenberg, Carolyn Ryan, Paula Carlson, Alexandra Morehouse, Tim Burditt, Janie DeCelles, Heather Evans, John Wilson, Doug Hansen, Kate Wolford, Judy Glasser, Margaret Adrain, Jack and Mable Collins, Saul Fern, Jim Hopkins, Elizabeth Garno, Rev. Rebecca Spencer, Lloyd and Gloria Hood and the Rhode Island Special Olympics family. To Arthur Matteson, George Egan, Al Gunther, Gus Anthony, Larry West, Calvin Brainard, Rod Crafts, George deLodzia, Roger Hale, Carol Knauff, Ed Strow, Dick Butler, Ron Stenning, Phil Noel, Al Verrecchia, Paul Choquette, David Sprinkle and Roy Ballentine. Thank you for the love, the faith, the wisdom and the encouragement you've given me every day of my life. To the many folks who helped pull the book together—

to Rep. Patrick J. Kennedy, America's youngest congressman, whose leadership shall prove to be the stuff of legend and whose early assistance and support on this project were invaluable. To those who took the time, amidst a mountain of worthy demands, to reflect on their lives and experiences and share a thought with us. To publisher Michael Cader for his belief and support of the vision. To my friend Larry Berman, press secretary to Congressman Kennedy and the embodiment of the Theta Chi heritage of the "Helping Hand." To my mom, who spent countless hours researching and recording addresses and building databases. To my assistant editor Olympian Jamie Koven and to David Filippone, Lorraine Bandoni, Paul Garrido, Adam Saffer, Gail Hochman, Tom Peckham, Nicole Hynes, Brad Telford, Verity Liljedahl, and Mickey Ackerman, each of whom were immensely helpful in the laborious process of finding and communicating with people and in so many other activities required to make the book a reality.

It gives me pleasure to recognize here all the people who have had a role in advancing the mission of RACE for Quality of Management. I created RACE in 1992 to help Rhode Island businesses improve their competitiveness and in so doing, to contribute to an improved economy and quality of life in our state. It was founded on the principles of leadership, shared learning and teamwork and the belief that if we could learn, apply and teach the tools of Total Quality Management then we might establish a new paradigm of leadership and cooperation within our state. The RACE team sponsors numerous programs, most notably the Rhode Island Quality Awards program, modeled after the Baldrige National Quality Award and considered to be among the most effective programs in the nation. The team's hard work and belief have withstood the test of time and have produced a cooperation knowing no boundaries and resulting in extraordinary gains in our collective spirit.

# The Rhode Island Foundation

I am pleased and proud to support the mission of the Rhode Island Foundation. It is one of the oldest, largest and most effective of the more than 400 independently operated community foundations benefiting the nation's cities, states, and regions. The Foundation sponsors programs and projects meeting the widest imaginable range of human needs, from arts and education to health and economic development. Founded in 1916, it is guided by a diverse board of community leaders, chosen for their sensitivity to and knowledge of Rhode Island's needs. The Foundation works with more than a thousand Rhode Island philanthropists, helping them meet their charitable goals. Royalties given to the Rhode Island Foundation will be used to recognize and support leadership, excellence and service in the Rhode Island community.

My grandmother told me that
every good thing I do helps
some human being in the
world. I believed her fifty
years ago and I still do.

Joy, Maya Angelou

I
My grandmother told me that every good thing I do helps some human being in the world. I believed her fifty years ago and I still do.

—MAYA ANGELOU
*Poet*

The most important thing I know
(and do) is that I am my kid's mom.

Laura Schlessinger

**2**
The most important thing I know (and do) is that I am my kid's mom.

—LAURA SCHLESSINGER
*Radio talk show host*

Excellence is Not a destination you arrive
at... It is the benchmark for your journey.

*Earvin Magic Johnson*

**3**
Excellence is not a destination you arrive at ... It is the benchmark for your journey.

—EARVIN "MAGIC" JOHNSON
*Basketball great*

# *Martina Navratilova*

Katharine Hepburn once told me
" It's not what you do in life,
it's what you finish." But many
people don't even start, because they
are afraid of failure. To me the only
failure is when you don't even try.
So set your path, be brave,
do your best and _smile_, because you
are doing all of the above.

Martina NAVRATILOVA

**4**

Katharine Hepburn once told me, "It's not what you do in life, it's what you finish!" But many people don't even start, because they are afraid of failure. To me the only failure is when you don't even try. So set your path, be brave, do your best and *smile*, because you are doing all of the above.

—MARTINA NAVRATILOVA
*Tennis Hall of Famer*

RICHARD A. GEPHARDT
DEMOCRATIC LEADER

I try to live by the Golden Rule — — to always accord others the same dignity, decency, and respect that we all want in our own lives. In my experience, you can achieve much more by bringing others along with you.

Dick Gephardt

5
I try to live by the Golden Rule—to always accord others the same dignity, decency, and respect that we all want in our own lives. In my experience, you can achieve much more by bringing others along with you.

—Richard A. Gephardt
*Democratic leader, United States Congress*

True excellence requires a worthy dream, a good idea of how to realize it, and the the courage to risk failure to achieve it.

Bill Clinton

6
True excellence requires a worthy dream, a good idea of how to realize it, and the courage to risk failure to achieve it.

—BILL CLINTON
*42nd President of the United States*

Eighty years ago, at the impressionable age of 12, I was thrilled to be "Sworn in" as a member of the Boy Scouts of America! I raised my right hand in the Scout Sign and took the Scout Oath promising "To do my best" to live by this Oath and its 12 individual Scout Laws. Now at the age of 92, with the world full of negatives, I realize the all-positive approach of these ideals and I fully appreciate how they are still guiding my life.

Thank you Boy Scouts!

H. Cushman Anthony

7
Eighty years ago, at the impressionable age of 12, I was thrilled to be "sworn in" as a member of the Boy Scouts of America! I raised my right hand in the Scout Sign and took the Scout Oath promising "To do my best" to live by this Oath and its twelve individual Scout Laws. Now at the age of 92, with the world full of negatives, I realize the all-positive approach of these ideals and I fully appreciate how they are still guiding my life. Thank you Boy Scouts!

—H. Cushman Anthony
*Boy Scout pioneer*

**Edward C Johnson 3d**
Chairman of the Board
Chief Executive Officer

Excellence begins by doing something you have a natural talent for and enjoy. You become totally absorbed in the work. Attention and involvement in all the details lead to success.

Red Johnson

8
Excellence begins by doing something you have a natural talent for and enjoy. You become totally absorbed in the work. Attention and involvement in all the details lead to success.

—EDWARD C JOHNSON 3D
*Chairman of the Board, Fidelity Investments*

The most important expression
of excellence is excellence
in choosing the actions
in which to excel.

Alvin & Heidi Toffler

**9**
The most important expression of excellence is excellence in choosing the actions in which to excel.

—ALVIN AND HEIDI TOFFLER
*Futurists*

General Colin L. Powell, USA (Retired)

You have Achieved excellence as a leader when people will follow you anywhere, if only out of curiosity.

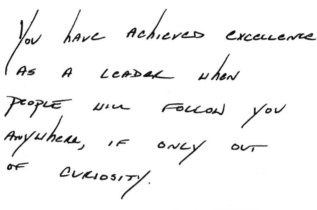

General, USA (Ret)

You have achieved excellence as a leader when people will follow you anywhere, if only out of curiosity.

—COLIN L. POWELL
*Four-star General; former Chairman, Joint Chiefs of Staff*

Spelman College

Johnnetta B. Cole, President

I think the most profound expression of education is action — — action in the interest of helping to heal what ails our communities, our nation and our world.

Johnnetta Cole

II

**11**
I think the most profound expression of education is action—action in the interest of helping to heal what ails our communities, our nation and our world.

—JOHNNETTA B. COLE
*President, Spelman College*

The vigorous pursuit of excellence remains a full-time job; often offering few benefits beyond personal satisfaction; providing no compensation other than rewards banked by the spirit; and allowing little opportunity for vacation. It is a job, however, for which anyone can qualify, regardless of age, gender, race, creed, background or lifestyle. It is a career choice I highly recommend.

Christine Whit

**12**

The vigorous pursuit of excellence remains a full-time job, often offering few benefits beyond personal satisfaction, providing no compensation other than rewards banked by the spirit, and allowing little opportunity for vacation. It is a job, however, for which anyone can qualify regardless of age, gender, race, creed, background or lifestyle. It is a career choice I highly recommend.

—CHRISTINE TODD WHITMAN
*Governor of New Jersey*

**P. S.**

In order to reach
excellence around the
world with many fragile
areas we need world
leaders to understand
History. So many don't!
History is critical to
learn how to solve
difficult worldwide
problems.

Pierre Salinger

**13**

In order to reach excellence around the world with many fragile areas we need world leaders to understand history. So many don't! History is critical to learn how to solve difficult worldwide problems.

—PIERRE SALINGER
*Press Secretary to President John F. Kennedy; journalist*

**Buzz Aldrin**
Astronaut

NO DREAM IS TOO HIGH
FOR THOSE WITH THEIR
EYES IN THE SKY

**14**
No dream is too high for those with their eyes in the sky.

—Buzz Aldrin
*Astronaut*

To acquire knowledge, one must study; but to acquire wisdom, one must observe.

Marilyn vos Savant

**15**
To acquire knowledge, one must study; but to acquire wisdom,
one must observe.

—MARILYN VOS SAVANT
*Columnist*

I have always been grateful
for the tolerance my parents
showed for the ambition I had
for a strange profession.
Not many young people have
the obsession to draw a comic
strip, and it was a difficult
ambition to understand, but they
never tried to discourage me, or
point me in a different direction.

Charles M. Schulz

**16**
I have always been grateful for the tolerance my parents showed for the ambition I had for a strange profession. Not many young people have the obsession to draw a comic strip, and it was a difficult ambition to understand, but they never tried to discourage me, or point me in a different direction.

—CHARLES M. SCHULZ
*Cartoonist*

# Carnegie Endowment for International Peace

Morton I. Abramowitz
*President*

My mother, a Jewish immigrant from Lithuania, used to tell her seven kids "all my children are excellent. What's the big deal. Go do some good in the world and I'll be impressed."

Morton Abramowitz

**17**

My mother, a Jewish immigrant from Lithuania, used to tell her seven kids, "All my children are excellent. What's the big deal. Go do some good in the world and I'll be impressed."

—MORTON I. ABRAMOWITZ
*International-relations leader*

*Corcoran Department of History*

Excellence and equity are inseparable – a good society cannot have one without the other.

Any society that abandons either is imperfect.

*Julian Bond*

**18**

Excellence and equity are inseparable—a good society cannot have one without the other. Any society that abandons either is imperfect.

—JULIAN BOND
*Civil rights pioneer*

Excellence doesn't happen without dedication and hard work or without always taking the time and effort to cross the "Ts" and dot the "is".

I always try and remember my father's advice: Prior Preparation Prevents Poor Performance!

Jim Baker

Excellence doesn't happen without dedication and hard work or without always taking the time and effort to cross the "t's" and dot the "i's." I always try and remember my father's advice: Prior Preparation Prevents Poor Performance!

—JAMES A. BAKER, III
*Former Secretary of State*

Do what you can to show you care about other people, and you will make our world a better place.

Rosalynn Carter

20
Do what you can to show you care about other people, and you will make our world a better place.

—ROSALYNN CARTER
*Former First Lady*

Elaine L. Chao
President and Chief Executive Officer

The pursuit of excellence
is a continuous process
through life. Enjoy
the pursuit.

E.L. Chao

**21**
The pursuit of excellence is a continuous process through life.
Enjoy the pursuit.

—ELAINE L. CHAO
*President and CEO, United Way of America*

# Peter Vidmar

Some of my fondest memories in sport were a result of failure, injuries, setbacks, or mistakes. I learned far more about myself and gained more character in those difficult times, than I ever did when success came easily.

*Pete Vidmar*

**22**

Some of my fondest memories in sport were a result of failure, injuries, setbacks, or mistakes. I learned far more about myself and gained more character in those difficult times than I ever did when success came easily.

—PETER VIDMAR
*Olympic Gold Medalist, Gymnastics*

## Kerri Strug

Work hard, be persistent and follow your dreams!

*Kerri Strug*

**23**
Work hard, be persistent and follow your dreams!

—KERRI STRUG
*Olympic Gold Medalist, Gymnastics*

Respect Children. But also ask for respect from your Children. Trust yourself. You know more than you think you do.

Ben Spock

**24**
Respect children. But also ask for respect from your children.
Trust yourself. You know more than you think you do.

—BENJAMIN SPOCK
*Pediatrician; child-rearing authority*

my Parents always
believed that I was THE
BEST! With thoughts like
that behind you, it's impossible
not to strive for excellence.
No one wants to disappoint
their Parents.

*Eileen Ford*

**25**

My parents always believed that I was The Best! With thoughts like that behind you, it's impossible not to strive for excellence. No one wants to disappoint their parents.

—EILEEN FORD
*Founder, Ford Modeling Agency*

The old Latins have said "Historia est magistra vitae" – History is a teacher of life. And I say that the future of the world is in the hands of children. If we don't dig out and show them the mistakes that were made in the past and that are being committed nowdays, there will be a small chance of the future being better. And the worldwide peace and tolerance will still be just a great dream of humanity.

Zlata Filipović

The old Latins have said, "Historia est magistra vitae"—history is a teacher of life. And I say that the future of the world is in the hands of children. If we don't dig out and show them the mistakes that were made in the past and that are being committed nowadays, there will be a small chance of the future being better. And the worldwide peace and tolerance will still be just a great dream of humanity.

—ZLATA FILIPOVIĆ
*Author,* Zlata's Diary: A Child's Life in Sarajevo

Humility is the mother of all virtues,
courage the father, integrity the child
and wisdom the grandchild.

Stephen R. Covey

**27**
Humility is the mother of all virtues, courage the father, integrity the child and wisdom the grandchild.

—STEPHEN R. COVEY
*Author; leadership authority*

The most important thing a woman can do is ask herself what she really wants and then go for it! Despite the risks, the gains are worth the costs. Along with personal and political power come confidence, optimism, a sense of community and self-worth, the feeling of living lovingly, honestly and well. When you add your voice to others, we begin collectively to answer the question what women want, we become stronger and more determined to get it.

*Patricia Ireland*

28

28

The most important thing a woman can do is ask herself what she really wants and then go for it! Despite the risks, the gains are worth the costs. Along with personal and political power come confidence, optimism, a sense of community and self-worth, the feeling of living lovingly, honestly and well. When you add your voice to others, we begin collectively to answer the question what women want, we become stronger and more determined to get it.

—PATRICIA IRELAND
*Women's rights advocate*

*"I cried everyday for a new pair of shoes until I saw the man with no feet."*

Florence Griffith Joyner
"Flo Jo"

**29**
"I cried everyday for a new pair of shoes until I saw the man with no feet."

—FLORENCE GRIFFITH JOYNER
*Olympic Gold Medalist, Track and Field*

to excell is to reach your own highest dream. But you must also help others, where and when you can, to reach theirs. Personal gain is empty if you do not feel you have positively touched another's life.

Barbara Walters

30
To excel is to reach your own highest dream. But you must also help others, where and when you can, to reach theirs. Personal gain is empty if you do not feel you have positively touched another's life.

—BARBARA WALTERS
*Journalist*

Service is the rent
we each pay for living.
It is not something to do
in your spare time; it is
the very purpose of life.

Marian Wright Edelman

**31**
Service is the rent we each pay for living. It is not something to
do in your spare time; it is the very purpose of life.

—MARIAN WRIGHT EDELMAN
*Founder, Children's Defense Fund*

I've always found these words by Daniel Webster, whose seat I hold in the Senate, especially inspiring: "Let us develop the resources of our land, call forth its powers, build up its institutions, promote all its great interests, and see whether we also in our day and generation may not perform something worthy to be remembered."

Edward M. Kennedy

I've always found these words by Daniel Webster, whose seat I hold in the Senate, especially inspiring: "Let us develop the resources of our land, call forth its powers, build up its institutions, promote all its great interests, and see whether we also in our day and generation may not perform something worthy to be remembered."

—EDWARD M. KENNEDY
*United States Senator*

" When you're not practicing,
remember, someone, somewhere is
practicing and when you two meet,
given roughly equal ability, he'll
win."
        I never wanted to lose because
I hadn't made effort. So, it has
been a lifetime of work, work,
work — which is, as Conrad said,
" The sustaining illusion of an independent
existence."

*Bill Bradley*

Bill Bradley
United States Senator

**33**

"When you're not practicing, remember, someone, somewhere is practicing and when you two meet, given roughly equal ability, he'll win." I never wanted to lose because I hadn't made effort. So, it has been a lifetime of work, work, work—which is, as Conrad said, "the sustaining illusion of an independent existence."

—BILL BRADLEY
*United States Senator; basketball Hall of Famer*

Champions are not made on
the Track or field; Champions are
made by the things one accomplishes
and the way one uses his/her
abilities in everyday life situations
one must approach a situation
with straight-ahead focus as
well as have peripheral focus
in order to arrive at the
best decision.

*Bob Beamon*

**34**
Champions are not made on the track or field; Champions are made by the things one accomplishes and the way one uses his/her abilities in everyday life situations. One must approach a situation with straight-ahead focus as well as have peripheral focus in order to arrive at the best decision.

—BOB BEAMON
*Olympic Gold Medalist, Track and Field*

# George Bush

Leadership to me means duty, honor, country. It means character and it means listening from time to time

*G. Bush*

**35**
Leadership to me means duty, honor, country. It means character and it means listening from time to time.

—GEORGE BUSH
*41st President of the United States*

**Orit Gadiesh**
Chairman of the Board

To achieve excellence, you
must stick to your own
TRUE North - your own core
principles and values. If you do -
- it will guide you as you make
decisions on the margin. It will
give you the courage to always
find the truth, look it square in
the eye and stick to it even when
it's hard. If you use and project
the power that comes with convictions
then no matter what you face,
you will be unique and remarkable.

Orit Gadiesh

## 36

To achieve excellence, you must stick to your own True North—
your own core principles and values. If you do, it will guide you
as you make decisions on the margin. It will give you the courage
to always find the truth, look it square in the eye and stick to it
even when it's hard. If you use and project the power that comes
with convictions, then no matter what you face, you will be
unique and remarkable.

—ORIT GADIESH
*Management consultant*

**WENDY'S INTERNATIONAL, INC.**

**R. DAVID THOMAS**
Senior Chairman of the Board & Founder

America is the greatest
Country in the world. You can
be anything you want to be
within the laws of God and Man.
You can make your dreams
come true if you work hard,
stay focused on your goal
and give back to the community
that supports you.

Dave Thomas

America is the greatest country in the world. You can be anything you want to be within the laws of God and man. You can make your dreams come true if you work hard, stay focused on your goal and give back to the community that supports you.

—R. DAVID THOMAS
*Senior Chairman and Founder, Wendy's International*

President          Republic of South Africa

The real heroes are men and women
who are friends of the poorest of the poor.

Mandela

38

The real heroes are men and women who are friends of the poorest of the poor.

—NELSON MANDELA
*President of the Republic of South Africa*

Aim High! There is little virtue in easy victory. If you are completely confident of success on a big challenge - then why start? - maybe you should be trying something more difficult. But being sensible is important too. There are two aspects to achievement - reaching your goal and getting safely back home again. One is incomplete without the other!

Ed Hillary

Sir Edmund Hillary

**39**

Aim high! There is little virtue in easy victory! If you are completely confident of success on a big challenge—then why start?—maybe you should be trying something more difficult. But being sensible is important too. There are two aspects to achievement—reaching your goal and getting safely back home again. One is incomplete without the other!

—SIR EDMUND HILLARY
*First to reach the summit of Mount Everest*

## ROBERT SCHULLER

Excellence! The attitude generates enthusiasm, attracts top people, & becomes the basis for real optimism.

It will generate powerful self esteem without falling into the trap of perfectionism.

For me its spiritual, God gives me the dream & I owe him a finished achievement worthy of a gift t him. *Bob Schuller*

Excellence! The attitude generates enthusiasm, attracts top people, and becomes the basis for real optimism. It will generate powerful self–esteem without falling into the trap of perfectionism. For me it's spiritual. God gives me the dream and I owe him a finished achievement worthy of a gift to him.

—ROBERT SCHULLER
*Religious leader*

Excellence exists in many dimensions --
ideas, actions, inventions, leadership, moral
awareness. No one is or can be excellent
on all of these dimensions but everyone should
strive to be excellent on some -- your aim
the sky, your goal the star

*Lester C. Thurow*

41

**41**

Excellence exists in many dimensions—ideas, actions, inventions, leadership, moral awareness. No one is or can be excellent in all of these dimensions but everyone should strive to be excellent in some—Your aim the sky, your goal the star.

—LESTER C. THUROW
*Management authority*

## RUBY BRIDGES
### A CHILD OF COURAGE,
### A WOMAN OF DETERMINATION

Don't follow the path.
Go where there is no path
& begin the trail.
When you start a new
trail equipped with courage
strength and conviction the
only thing that can stop you
is you!

Ruby Bridges
Civil Rights Pioneer

42

**42**

Don't follow the path. Go where there is no path and begin the trail. When you start a new trail equipped with courage, strength and conviction, the only thing that can stop you is you!

—RUBY BRIDGES
*Civil rights pioneer*

UNITED STATES SENATOR

BEN NIGHTHORSE CAMPBELL
COLORADO

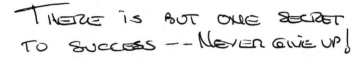

THERE IS BUT ONE SECRET
TO SUCCESS -- NEVER GIVE UP!

*Ben Nighthorse Campbell*

**43**
There is but one secret to success—never give up!

—BEN NIGHTHORSE CAMPBELL
*United States Senator*

*Andress /*

Love what you do. Believe in your instincts. And you'd better be able to pick yourself up and brush yourself off every day.

While life is not always fair, it is manageable. It is a matter of attitude and confidence.

**44**

Love what you do. Believe in your instincts. And you'd better be able to pick yourself up and brush yourself off every day. While life is not always fair, it is manageable. It is a matter of attitude and confidence.

—MARIO ANDRETTI
*Automobile racing champion*

THE SECRETARY-GENERAL

Ever since my youth I have been inspired whenever I contemplate the NILE, the river-god my ancestors who worshipped. The Nile flows on indifferent to mere events. It carries a message from the heart of Africa our common home. It brings life to all who live near its banks. It contributes its waters to the Mediterranean and the great civilizations which surround its shores. And ultimately it flows and merges with all the world's oceans which link every continent and all people of our planet. To me, it is a constant reminder of our common humanity.

45

**45**

Ever since my youth I have been inspired whenever I contemplate the Nile, the river-god my ancestors worshiped. The Nile flows on indifferent to mere events. It carries a message from the heart of Africa, our common home. It brings life to all who live near its banks. It contributes its water to the Mediterranean and the great civilizations which surround its shores. And ultimately it flows and merges with all the world's oceans which link every continent and all people of our planet. To me, it is a constant reminder of our common humanity.

—BOUTROS BOUTROS-GHALI
*Secretary General of the United Nations*

**NORMAN LAMM**
President

The achievement of excellence requires great effort, much planning, and even more time.

But, in the long run, mediocrity costs more, drains your energy, and wastes even more time than it takes to do things right.

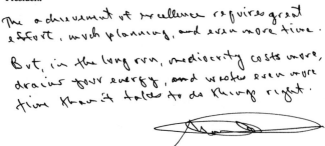

**46**

The achievement of excellence requires great effort, much planning, and even more time. But, in the long run, mediocrity costs more, drains your energy, and wastes even more time than it takes to do things right.

—NORMAN LAMM
*President, Yeshiva University*

In the "Marathon of Life", success in life calls for dedication, to the goal, perseverance, compassion for my fellow man + in Faith in God!

John A Kelley

**47**
In the "Marathon of Life," success in life calls for dedication to the goal, perseverance, compassion for my fellow man and faith in God!

—JOHN A. KELLEY
*Sixty-one–time participant in the Boston Marathon (two–time winner)*

*Office of the Chairman*

Excellence is recognizable to most people. To fully appreciate its magnificence, however, one must study how it got there — then you feel the tingle.

*[signature]*

**48**

Excellence is recognizable to most people. To fully appreciate its magnificence, however, one must study how it got there—*then* you feel the tingle.

—JANE ALEXANDER
*Actor; Chairman, National Endowment for the Arts*

# MILTON FRIEDMAN

There is no such thing as
a free lunch. The search
for one through government
is ruining our society.

Milton Friedman

**49**
There is no such thing as a free lunch. The search for one through government is ruining our society.

—MILTON FRIEDMAN
*Nobel Prize winner in Economic Sciences*

Cold Spring Harbor Laboratory

Excellence demands the pursuit of seemingly
unattainable goals. Those teachers and schools
that truly succeed are those which inspire
their students to move beyond the expectation of
conventional wisdom

James D. Watson

50

Excellence demands the pursuit of seemingly unattainable goals. Those teachers and schools that truly succeed are those which inspire their students to move beyond the expectation of conventional wisdom.

—JAMES D. WATSON
*Nobel Prize winner in Physiology or Medicine; co–discoverer DNA*

LEONARD A. SCHLESINGER
*George Fisher Baker, Jr. Professor
of Business Administration*

Ultimately all you will have left at the end of the day are your name and your reputation. Invest in them wisely and you and others will simultaneously reap the rewards.

Len Schlesinger

**51**

Ultimately all you will have left at the end of the day are your name and your reputation. Invest in them wisely and you and others will simultaneously reap the rewards.

—LEONARD A. SCHLESINGER
*Management authority*

# COSMOPOLITAN

Helen Gurley Brown, Editor

You don't have to think
too much about "excellence"....
that sounds kind of fancy.
Just do the work in front of
you ... grubby as it seems
at the time ... the very best
you can and it will probably
lead to excellence

Helen Gurley Brown

52
You don't have to think too much about "excellence"—that sounds kind of fancy. Just do the work in front of you—grubby as it seems at the time—the very best you can and it will probably *lead* to excellence.

—HELEN GURLEY BROWN
*Founder,* Cosmopolitan

THE JOURNEY IS THE
REWARD

**Great White Shark Enterprises, Inc.**

**53**
The journey is the reward.

—GREG NORMAN
*Golf champion*

UNIVERSITY OF NOTRE DAME

*From the desk of ...*
**REV. THEODORE M. HESBURGH, C.S.C.**
President Emeritus

Every young person
in America should
believe that with
God's help, he or
she can make a great
difference for good—
both in America
and throughout the
world.

Father Ted
Hesburgh
cr.

**54**

Every young person in America should believe that with God's help, he or she can make a great difference for good—both in America and throughout the world.

—REVEREND THEODORE M. HESBURGH
*President Emeritus, University of Notre Dame*

**PRIME MINISTER**

Life is a constant struggle. It is the story of how each person copes with the difficulties and challenges which arise.

It is important to work hard, have faith, patience and persevere in overcoming odds.

It is important to build relationships on the principles of love, loyalty and honour.

Life, for me, is about giving. If by one small act I can make someone happy, it brightens up my day.

Benazir Bhutto.

**55**

Life is a constant struggle. It is the story of how each person copes with the difficulties and challenges which arise. It is important to work hard, have faith, patience and persevere in overcoming odds. It is important to build relationships on the principles of love, loyalty and honor. Life, for me, is about giving. If by one small act I can make someone happy, it brightens up my day.

—BENAZIR BHUTTO
*Prime Minister of Pakistan*

Persrevere—don't be so
stuffy you can't laugh at
yourself!

James S. Brady

Persevere—don't be so stuffy you can't laugh at yourself!

—JAMES S. BRADY
*Press Secretary to President Ronald Reagan;*
*advocate for the rights of the disabled*

. To reach your goals work hard .
participate practice and do the
best you can

. Joseph p connors

57

57
To reach your goals work hard, participate, practice, and do the best you can.

—JOSEPH P. CONNORS
*Special Olympics athlete; Eagle Scout*

For almost thirty
years Special Olympics
athletes have been
teaching about excellence
and leadership. They
have taught me
what it means to
work together as
friends, & give of our
hearts, minds, and
physical abilities to a
great unifying cause
The pursuit of
happiness discovery caring
transcendence.
That is Excellence
Eunice Kennedy Shriver

58

58
For almost thirty years, Special Olympics athletes have been teaching about excellence and leadership. They have taught me what it means to work together as friends, to give of our hearts, minds, and physical abilities to a great unifying cause. The pursuit of happiness, discovery, caring and transcendence—that is excellence.

EUNICE KENNEDY SHRIVER
*Founder, Special Olympics International*

Anything in life is possible
if you make it happen, and
its never too late.

Jack La Lanne

**59**
Anything in life is possible if you make it happen. And it's never too late.

—JACK LA LANNE
*Fitness pioneer*

# BONNIE BLAIR════

## OLYMPIC GOLD MEDALIST

Acheiving your personal best is
all one can ask of themselves. If the
results are first, fourth or thirtieth,
and it is the best you have ever done,
then that is something to be proud of.

*Bonnie Blair*

**60**

Achieving your personal best is all one can ask of themselves. If the results are first, fourth or thirtieth, and it is the best you have ever done, then that is something to be proud of.

—BONNIE BLAIR
*Olympic Gold Medalist, Speed Skating*

"If Your Actions create a Legacy that inspires others to Dream More, Learn More, Do More and Become More, then, You are an excellent Leader."

— Dolly Parton

**61**
"If your actions create a legacy that inspires others to dream more, learn more, do more and become more, then, you are an excellent leader."

—DOLLY PARTON
*Singer; actor*

# Ted Williams

I've found in life
the more you practice
the better You get,
if you want something
enough + work hard to get
it Your chances of success
are much greater

Ted Williams

**62**

I've found in life the more you practice the better you get. If you want something enough and work hard to get it your chances of success are much greater.

—TED WILLIAMS
*Baseball Hall of Famer*

DANCE
THEATRE
*of*
HARLEM

DISCIPLINE, SELF-ESTEEM AND SELF-RELIANCE
ARE THREE INGREDIENTS NECESSARY IN THE PURSUIT
OF EXCELLENCE. FOR SOMEONE LIKE MYSELF
WHO HAS HAD TO OVERCOME HARDSHIP,
ADVERSITY AND BARRIERS OF MANY KINDS,
THESE INGREDIENTS, TOGETHER WITH A DETERMINATION
TO FULFILL MY DREAMS HAVE ENABLED ME
TO ACCOMPLISH THINGS THAT (WAS TOLD) COULD
NOT BE DONE. OUT OF THIS RECIPE FOR
EXCELLENCE, DANCE THEATRE OF HARLEM
HAS BECOME A BEACON OF SUCCESS
TO GUIDE YOUNG PEOPLE EVERYWHERE.

*Arthur Mitchell*

63

**63**

Discipline, self-esteem, and self-reliance are three ingredients necessary in the pursuit of excellence. For someone like myself who has had to overcome hardship, adversity and barriers of many kinds, these ingredients, together with a determination to fulfill my dreams, have enabled me to accomplish things that I was told could not be done. Out of this recipe for excellence, Dance Theatre of Harlem has become a beacon of success to guide young people everywhere.

—ARTHUR MITCHELL
*Founder, President, and Artistic Director, Dance Theater of Harlem*

## J. Carter Brown

*Director Emeritus, National Gallery of Art*

The "habitual contemplation of greatness" — in Alfred North Whiteheads rubic — must inform and inspire us. Greatness — and excellence — are best and most lastingly communicated through the arts.

J. Carter Brown

The "habitual contemplation of greatness"—in Alfred North Whitehead's rubric—must inform and inspire us. Greatness—and excellence—are best and most lastingly communicated through the arts.

—J. CARTER BROWN
*Director Emeritus, National Gallery of Art*

We become what we expect
to become. Greatness can be
achieved only if we expect it
from ourselves & from others!

Jim Ericson

**65**
We become what we expect to become. Greatness can be achieved only if we expect it from ourselves and from others!

—JAMES D. ERICSON
*President, Northwestern Mutual Life*

*Never get into the thick of thin things!*

66
Never get into the thick of thin things!

—ROBERT DUANE BALLARD
*Oceanographer (found the wreck of the* Titanic*)*

Excellence is the eternal quest. We achieve it by living up to our highest intellectual standards and our finest moral intuitions.

In seeking excellence, take life seriously — but never yourself.

*Arthur Schlesinger, Jr.*

**67**

Excellence is the eternal quest. We achieve it by living up to our highest intellectual standards and our finest moral intuitions. In seeking excellence, take life seriously—but never yourself.

—ARTHUR SCHLESINGER, JR.
*Pulitzer Prize winner in both History and Biography*

Tom Landry
Dallas, Texas

Thoughts on Excellence

"The quality of a man's life is in direct Proportion To his Commitment of excellence."

Tom Landry

68

"The quality of a man's life is in direct proportion to his commitment of excellence."

—TOM LANDRY
*Football Hall of Famer (coach)*

Incorporated

Having the courage to do things you are not an expert at, trying things that you are totally unsure about, having the courage to stick with it once you start and learning from every step that you take until your particular goal is reached. Even if your goal is never reached, it is a learning process that will enhance your life. Just remember, it is your decision to succeed or fail. No one else's

**69**

Having the courage to do things you are not an expert at, trying things that you are totally unsure about, having the courage to stick with it once you start and learning from every step that you take until your particular goal is reached. Even if your goal is never reached, it is a learning process that will enhance your life. Just remember, it is your decision to succeed or fail, no one else's.

—WALTER PAYTON
*Football Hall of Famer*

# Peggy Fleming Jenkins

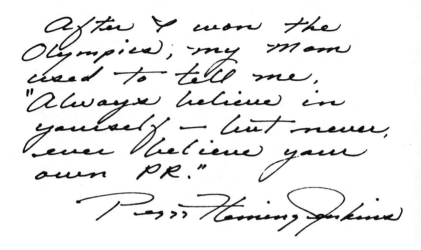

After I won the Olympics, my Mom used to tell me, "Always believe in yourself — but never, ever believe your own PR."

*Peggy Fleming Jenkins*

70
After I won the Olympics my mom used to tell me, "Always believe in yourself—but never, ever believe your own PR."

—PEGGY FLEMING JENKINS
*Olympic Gold Medalist, Figure Skating*

Excellence flows from many sources – a freedom of spirit that is open to both the old and the new, an attention to detail that shows respect for the often subtle and complex nature of the world, a willingness to learn and try again, a deep unease with things that are not right or which don't make sense, a capacity for introspection that leads to intellectual honesty with oneself and the world. Perhaps most important, true excellence is never tainted by incivility or arrogance towards others.

*Russell Hulse*

71
Excellence flows from many sources—a freedom of spirit that is open to both the old and the new, an attention to detail that shows respect for the often subtle and complex nature of the world, a willingness to learn and try again, a deep unease with things that are not right or which don't make sense, a capacity for introspection that leads to intellectual honesty with oneself and the world. Perhaps most important, true excellence is never tainted by incivility or arrogance towards others.

—RUSSELL HULSE
*Nobel Prize winner in Physics*

Because it hasn't been done
before, doesn't mean it can't
be done.

Those who are afraid
to make a mistake
will never make
a significant achievement.

Ted Hood

**72**
Because it hasn't been done before, doesn't mean it can't be done. Those who are afraid to make a mistake will never make a significant achievement.

—TED HOOD
*America's Cup winner*

GERALD R. FORD

*Personal excellence can be achieved by a visionary goal, thorough planning, dedicated execution and total follow through.*

*Gerald R. Ford*
*38th President*

**73**
Personal excellence can be achieved by a visionary goal, thorough planning, dedicated execution and total follow through.

—GERALD R. FORD
*38th President of the United States*

My personal definition of success is — "peace of mind which is a direct result of self-satisfaction in knowing you made the effort to become the best of which you are capable."

Failure to prepare is preparing to fail.

Never try to be better than someone else, learn from others and never cease trying to the best that you can be.

John Wooden
UCLA (Ret.)

**74**

My personal definition of success is—"peace of mind which is a direct result of self-satisfaction in knowing you made the effort to become the best of which you are capable." Failure to prepare is preparing to fail. Never try to be better than someone else, learn from others and never cease trying to be the best you can be.

—JOHN R. WOODEN
*Basketball Hall of Famer (coach)*

I think that what's important is to base one's convictions on compassion for others and an ambitious sense of the possible, to commit to achieving ambitious goals, to plan carefully, to think and write clearly, to work hard, to learn constantly, and to progress always with integrity and sensitivity.

Wendy Kopp

## TEACH FOR AMERICA

**75**
I think that what's important is to base one's convictions on
compassion for others and an ambitious sense of the possible,
to commit to achieving ambitious goals, to plan carefully,
to think and write clearly, to work hard, to learn constantly,
and to progress always with integrity and sensitivity.

—WENDY KOPP
*Founder, Teach for America*

**ED**VENTURE HOLDINGS INC.
*Publisher of RELEASE 1.0 & Sponsor of PC Forum*

ESTHER DYSON
*President*

Always made new mistakes!

Esther D

**76**
Always make new mistakes!

—ESTHER DYSON
*Computer-industry leader*

The only thing that separates any of one of us from excellence is fear, and the opposite of fear is faith. I am careful not to confuse excellence with perfection. Excellence I can reach for, Perfection is God's business.

*Michael Fox*

77
The only thing that separates any one of us from excellence is fear, and the opposite of fear is faith. I am careful not to confuse excellence with perfection. Excellence I can reach for, perfection is God's business.

—MICHAEL J. FOX
*Actor*

Listen, Learn, Help, Lead
are the Keys to excellence
in leadership.
     you have to learn
everyday and set high
standards for yourself.

Newt
10 yrs

78

78
Listen, Learn, Help, Lead are the keys to excellence in leadership. You have to learn everyday and set high standards for yourself.

—NEWT GINGRICH
*Speaker of the United States House of Representatives*

*Make a start and sustain the effort!
Inspiration will follow with excellence
becoming the eventual result.*

*Take the time to listen to the trees.
That is where the Music is!*

*John Williams*

**79**
Make a start and sustain the effort! Inspiration will follow with excellence becoming the eventual result. Take the time to listen to the trees. That is where the music is!

—JOHN WILLIAMS
*Composer*

As the automobile commercial says, excellence is about the relentless search for perfection. It is not a search for "good enough". It is a search for perfection

Pete Peterson

80
As the automobile commercial says, excellence is about the relentless search for perfection. It is not a search for "good enough." It is a search for perfection.

—PETER G. PETERSON
*Business authority*

# The Museum of Modern Art

Agnes Gund
President

One gains through education and experience a passion for something special, something very important to ones life. For me it was the visual arts. Follow your passion and try to perfect all aspects of it. If you become excellent in that area you will be able to teach, support and extend your passion to others and for yourself. Do not try to follow what others may wish for you but follow your passion.

Agnes Gund.

One gains through education and experience a passion for something special, something very important to one's life. For me it was the visual arts. Follow your passion and try to perfect all aspects of it. If you become excellent in that area you will be able to teach, support and extend your passion to others and for yourself. Do not try to follow what others may wish for you, but follow your passion.

—AGNES GUND
*President, The Museum of Modern Art*

I often use a quote by Edward Everett Hale which best sums up my philosophy, "I am only one, but still I am one. I cannot do everything, but still I can do something. And because I cannot do everything, I will not refuse to do the something I can do."

If everyone would take this to heart, most of our problems would be solved & there would be no need for organizations such as Mothers Against Drunk Driving

Candace Lightner

82

I often use a quote by Edward Everett Hale which best sums up my philosophy: "I am only one, but still I am one. I cannot do everything, but still I can do something. And because I cannot do everything, I will not refuse to do the something I can do." If everyone would take this to heart, most of our problems would be solved and there would be no need for organizations such as Mothers Against Drunk Driving.

—CANDACE LIGHTNER
*Founder, Mothers Against Drunk Driving*

Every individual matters, non-human
as well as human. Every individual
has a role to play. Every
individual makes a difference.

We cannot live through a single
day without making an impact
on the world around us. And we
all have free choice - what
sort of difference do we want
to make? Do we want to make
the world around us a
better place? Or not?

Jane Goodall

© Mark Maglio 1990

"Fifi fishing for termites"
derived from Hugo Van Lawick, 1964 photo.

83
Every individual matters, non-human as well as human. Every individual has a role to play. Every individual makes a difference. We cannot live through a single day without making an impact on the world around us. And we all have free choice—what sort of difference do we want to make? Do we want to make the world around us a better place? Or not?

—JANE GOODALL
*Wildlife researcher*

Leadership means having the courage to take decisions, not for easy headlines in 10 days but for a better country in 10 years.

Brian Mulroney

**84**
Leadership means having the courage to take decisions, not for easy headlines in ten days but for a better country in ten years.

—BRIAN MULRONEY
*Former Prime Minister of Canada*

You are capable of more than you know. Choose a goal that seems right for you and strive to be the best, however hard the path. Aim high. Behave honorably. Prepare to be alone at times, and to endure failure. Persist! The world needs all you can give.

Edw. O. Wilson

**85**

You are capable of more than you know. Choose a goal that seems right for you and strive to be the best, however hard the path. Aim high. Behave honorably. Prepare to be alone at times, and to endure failure. Persist! The world needs all you can give.

—EDWARD O. WILSON
*Two-time Pulitzer Prize winner; biologist*

An innate, searching curiosity
about all around us —
— what do we _not_ know?
— how can we do it differently?
— how can we do it _better_?
is at the heart of excellence.

Then, human progress and
excellence comes when someone
goes beyond "why" to "why _not_?"

John Glenn

**86**
An innate, searching curiosity about all around us—

> What do we *not know*?
> How can we do it *differently*?
> How can we do it *better*?
> is at the heart of excellence. Then, human progress and

excellence comes when someone goes beyond "why" to "why not?"

—JOHN GLENN
*United States Senator; astronaut*

ༀ། །ཇི་སྲིད་ནམ་མཁའ་གནས་པ་དང་།
།འགྲོ་བ་ཇི་སྲིད་གནས་གྱུར་པ།
།དེ་སྲིད་བདག་ནི་གནས་གྱུར་ནས།
།འགྲོ་བའི་སྡུག་བསྔལ་སེལ་བར་ཤོག །

87
For as long as space endures,
And for as long as living beings remain,
Until then may I, too, abide
To dispel the misery of the world.

—THE DALAI LAMA
*Exiled political and religous leader of the Tibetan people*

# MAN BECOMES THAT WHICH HE GAZES UPON.

George Harrison ॐ

from

(Life and Teachings of the
                    Masters of the East)

Friar Park Studio

88
Man becomes that which he gazes upon.

—GEORGE HARRISON
*Musician*

Excellence, to me, is the state of grace that can descend only when one tunes out all the world's clamor, listens to an inward voice one recognizes as wiser than one's own, and transcribes without fear.

Naomi Wolf

89
Excellence, to me, is the state of grace that can descend only when one tunes out all the world's clamor, listens to an inward voice one recognizes as wiser than one's own, and transcribes without fear.

—NAOMI WOLF
*Author; feminist leader*

**THE MOST REVEREND DESMOND M. TUTU, O.M.S.   D.D.   F.K.C.**
ANGLICAN ARCHBISHOP EMERITUS OF CAPE TOWN

"You are a very special person — become what you are"

*Desmond*

"Beloved, let us love one another, for love is of God — if there is this love among you,
then all will know that you are my disciples."

"You are a very special person—become what you are."

—ARCHBISHOP DESMOND M. TUTU
*Nobel Peace Prize winner*